OLIVER CROMWELL

J.R. Broome

2006

Gospel Standard Trust Publications
12(b) Roundwood Lane
Harpenden,
Hertfordshire AL5 3DD

ISBN 10 : 1-897837-69-0
ISBN 13 : 978-1-897837-69-6

Cover Picture :

Oliver Cromwell
Full length portrait attributed to Robert Walker
by kind permission of
the Cromwell Museum
Huntingdon

Printed by *Olive* Press
73 The Green
Stotfold
Hertfordshire
SG5 4AN

Oliver Cromwell

A copy of the portrait by Sir Peter Lely.

By kind permission of the Cromwell Museum

Huntingdon.

OLIVER CROMWELL

Cromwell was, and still is, a man whose name arouses much contention. He died in 1658 and was buried in Westminster Abbey. But at the time of the Restoration of the Monarchy in 1660 his body was removed from the Abbey, beheaded and hung at Tyburn, and it is believed that his last resting place is at the foot of Tyburn. Bitter hatred is still shown to him today. He is accused of being a hypocrite, a usurper, a dictator and a cruel tyrant who massacred the population of Drogheda in Ireland. But it is not impossible to demonstrate that he was a man of God; that what Christ said in his life was and is true of him, "If the world hate you, ye know that it hated me." The words of Christ are true of him, "God is not the God of the dead, but of the living." From a Christian position it is possible to believe that Cromwell lives today, and that he was one of the redeemed followers of the Lord Jesus and is now at the right hand of God in heaven, and that his dust lying at Tyburn waits in this earth the morning of the resurrection.

One of his earliest extant letters is dated 13th October, 1638, and is written from Ely in the Fens to his cousin Mrs. Oliver St. John in Essex. It reads:-

"I thankfully acknowledge your love in your kind remembrance of me upon this opportunity. Alas, you do too highly prize my lines, and my company. I may be ashamed to own your own expressions, considering how unprofitable I am, and the mean improvement of my talent.

Yet to honour my God by declaring what He hath done for my soul, in this I am confident, and I will be so. Truly, then, this I find: That He giveth springs in a dry and barren wilderness where no water is. I live (you know where) in Meschek, which they say signifies 'prolonging'; in Kedar which signifieth 'blackness': yet the Lord forsaketh me not.

Though He do prolong, yet He will (I trust) bring me to His tabernacle, to His resting place. My soul is with the congregation of the first-born, my body rests in hope; and if here I may honour my God, either by doing or by suffering, I shall be most glad.

Truly no poor creature hath more cause to put himself forth in the cause of his God than I. I have had plentiful wages beforehand; and I am sure that I shall never earn the least mite. The Lord accept me in His Son and give me to walk in the light, and give us to walk in the light, as He is in the light! He it is that enlighteneth our blackness, our darkness. I dare not say, He hideth his face from me. He giveth me to see light in His light. One beam in a dark place hath exceeding much refreshment in it; blessed be His Name for shining upon so dark a heart as mine! You know what my manner of life hath been. Oh, I lived in and loved darkness, and hated the light; I was a chief, the chief of sinners. This is true; I hated godliness, yet God had mercy on me. O the riches of His mercy! Praise Him for me. Pray for me, that He who hath begun a good work would perfect it in the day of Christ."[1]

How do we judge the contents of this letter ? Does it not echo the experience of John Bunyan? It speaks of the realities of Christian experience: 'One beam in a dark place hath exceeding much refreshment in it.' It reveals a man who knew what he had been: 'I hated godliness,' 'I lived in and loved darkness'. What he was: 'An unprofitable servant'. What he hoped for: 'Yet He will, I trust, bring me to His tabernacle, to His resting-place'. Poignant when one considers the future was the experiencing for him: 'My soul is with the congregation of the first-born, my body rests in hope, and if here I may honour my God either by doing or by suffering, I shall be most glad.'

The course of history shows how he did honour His God by doing and suffering; by doing in Parliament and on the battlefield and suffering many a blow from Royalist and Puritan. In April 1640, when he was forty-one he was returned as Member of Parliament for Cambridge to serve in what was known as the 'Short Parliament.' He had previously been in Parliament in 1628 as M.P. for Huntingdon and had made his maiden speech on 11th February,

1629. In March 1629 this Parliament was abruptly ended by Charles I and another not called until 13th April 1640. In this period Cromwell managed a small farm in the Fens, living at St. Ives and Ely and taking an interest in local affairs. (The letter just quoted comes from this period. It was a time of preparation). In April 1640 the call came to attend the House of Commons. The Short Parliament lasted only three weeks. But in November 1640 a second Parliament was called and Cromwell was again M.P. for Cambridge. This month of November 1640 marked the beginning of the key period in the history of Cromwell's life, extending from the opening of the 'Long Parliament' to his death on 3rd September, 1658, so brief a period comparatively, a mere eighteen years, and yet of such magnitude for himself and for his country.

The Long Parliament of the Civil Wars was finally dissolved by Cromwell's own hand in 1653, by which time it had become known as 'The Rump' on account of its decreasing numbers, through the secession of the Royalists and the exclusion by the army of the Presbyterian Party. In the years 1640-1642 Parliament tried to come to an agreement with the King but failed. The First Civil War began in August 1642, when Charles I raised his Standard at Nottingham, and lasted until 1646. It witnessed an indecisive battle at Edgehill in 1642 and two victories for Parliament in 1644 and 1645 at Marston Moor and Naseby. Oxford, the Royalist centre of control, finally surrendered in 1646, which ended the war. Charles I fled and gave himself up to the Scots. They in turn handed him over to Parliament. There then followed a struggle between the Army and the Long Parliament, until the Army took possession of the King and kept him at Hampton Court from where he escaped to Carisbrooke on the Isle of Wight. While at Carisbrooke he took advantage of the contention between Parliament and the Army to negotiate secretly with the Scots. In 1648, on his behalf, they invaded England, but were defeated by Cromwell at Preston. Before this, the Second Civil War, the Army leaders had held a prayer meeting at Windsor and it was felt after that meeting that 'Charles Stuart, that man of blood' must be called to account for his treacherous behaviour in starting a second war. The King was tried, and executed in Whitehall on 30th January, 1649. Cromwell then went to Ireland to suppress a Catholic insurrection there, when the Scots proclaimed Charles II as King of Scotland and he returned in 1650 to invade Scotland. He defeated the Scots at Dunbar on 3rd September that year and went on to Edinburgh where he had a serious illness and was delayed from further fighting until June of the following year. He then advanced up the east coast of Scotland but an army led by Charles II by-passed him on the west coast and crossed into England. The final victory came at Worcester, 3rd September, 1651, when Cromwell defeated this Army led by Charles II.

The Civil Wars were now over. In some respects it had been a three cornered fight. The Royalists had taken advantage of the differences between the Presbyterian and Independent sections of the Puritans. The Long Parliament had contained a large section of Presbyterians, while the New Model Army formed in 1645 under Sir Thomas Fairfax and Cromwell had been composed largely of Independents. The Presbyterians had been more favourable to the Monarchy than the Independents and had been willing to treat longer with the King. This was apparent among the Presbyterians in Scotland as well as in England and had led to the Scots supporting Charles I and Charles II, and to the sad sight of Puritan ministers of religion being present in both armies at Dunbar. The Scots were to realise their mistake in the years 1660-1685, when many thousands perished on the Moors of Scotland at the hand of the Stuarts, which family they had helped to keep on the English Throne.

In England after 1651, the Army faced the Parliament, the so-called 'Rump'. Throughout 1652 they disagreed over the payment and disbanding of the Army. In 1653 Cromwell went down to the House of Commons with some of his officers and forcibly ejected the fifty-three contentious members, all that remained of the Long Parliament of 1640. A Council of Army Officers was now set up to govern the country and a Parliament was made up of Puritan ministers and able men nominated by Cromwell and his Council of Officers. This Parliament eventually proved unsatisfactory. Religious fanaticism raised its head and it resigned its powers to Cromwell within a year. 'The Rump' had been the last constitutional part of the English Government machinery after the removal of the monarchy and the disintegration of the House of Lords. The Army leaders now produced a new constitution for the State called 'The Instrument of Government' by which Cromwell was appointed Lord Protector of the Commonwealth and governed with a Council of twenty-one advisers. From this time, 16th December, 1653, until his death on 3rd September, 1658, Cromwell virtually was the sole governor of England. He tried on two occasions in 1654 and 1656 to hand over some of his powers to an elected parliament – the first and second Protectorate Parliaments – but on each occasion the attempt failed, and when Cromwell died in 1658 the succession passed to his son Richard who was totally unfit to govern, and the result was the restoration of the Monarchy in 1660.

It is now possible, against this background, to consider Cromwell, first through his letters, then through his speeches, and finally to discuss some of the particular accusations made against him, such as the massacre at Drogheda and the charge of maliciously damaging church property.

The first letter is written to his brother-in-law, Colonel Valentine Walton, in 1644, just after the battle of Marston Moor. It describes the great victory near York and goes on to tell the Colonel of the death of his eldest son. In the letter Cromwell refers to his own sad loss in the spring of 1644; the death of his eldest son, Oliver. We see here gracious spiritual comfort given.

"Before York   5th July, 1644

Dear Sir,

It's our duty to sympathise in all mercies; that we may praise the Lord together in chastisement or trials, that so we may sorrow together. Truly England and the Church of God hath had a great favour from our Lord, in this great victory given unto us, such as the like never was since this war began. It had all the evidences of an absolute victory obtained by the Lord's blessing upon the godly party principally. We never charged but we routed the enemy. The left wing, which I commanded, being our own horse, saving a few Scots in our rear, beat all the Prince's horse (Prince Rupert). God made them as stubble to our swords. We charged their regiments of foot with our horse, routed all we charged. The particulars I cannot relate now; but I believe of twenty thousand the Prince hath not four thousand left. Give glory, all glory to God.

Sir, God hath taken away your eldest son by cannon shot. It broke his leg. We were necessitated to have it cut off, whereof he died.

Sir, you know my trials this way; but the Lord supported me with this, that the Lord took him into the happiness we all pant and live for. There is your precious child full of glory, to know sin nor sorrow any more. He was a gallant young man, exceeding gracious. God give you His comfort. Before his death he was so full of comfort that to Frank Russell and myself he could not express it, it was so great above his pain. Truly he was exceedingly beloved in the army of all that knew him. But few knew him; for he was a precious young man fit for God. You have cause to bless the Lord. He is a glorious saint in heaven; wherein you ought exceedingly to rejoice. Let this drink up your sorrow; seeing these are not feigned words to comfort you, but the thing is so real and undoubted a truth. You may do all things by the strength of Christ. Seek that and you shall easily bear your trial. Let this public mercy to the Church of God make you forget your private sorrow. The Lord be your strength. So prays your truly faithful and loving brother – Oliver Cromwell."[2]

The next two letters were written to inform the House of Commons of the great victories of Naseby and Dunbar. They are addressed to the Speaker, the Hon. William Lenthall, and contain much more than a mere account of the battle. After the battle of Naseby, Cromwell wrote:-

"Market Harborough   14th June, 1645

Sir,

...This is none other but the hand of God; and to Him alone belongs the glory, wherein none are to share with Him. The General served you well with all faithfulness and honour; and the best commendation I can give him is that, I dare say, he attributes all to God and would rather perish than assume to himself. Which is an honest and thriving way and yet as much for bravery may be given to him in this action, as to a man. Honest men served you faithfully in this action. Sir, they are trusty; I beseech you in the name of God not to discourage them. I wish this action may beget thankfulness and humility in all that are concerned in it. He that ventures his life for the liberty of his country, I wish he trust to God for the liberty of conscience and you for the liberty he fights for. In this he rests, who is, your most humble servant, Oliver Cromwell."[3]

After Dunbar, Cromwell wrote:-

"Dunbar   4th September 1650

Sir,

... Thus you have the prospect of one of the most signal mercies God hath done for England and His people this War. And now may it please you to give me leave of a few words. It is easy to say the Lord hath done this. It would do you good to see and hear our poor foot (soldiers) go up and down making their boast of God. But Sir, it is in your hands, and by these eminent mercies God puts it more into your hands, to give glory to Him; to improve your power and His blessings to His praise. We that serve you beg of you not to own us, but God alone; we pray you own His people more and more, for they are the chariots and horsemen of Israel. Disown yourselves but own your authority, and improve it to curb the proud and insolent, such as would disturb the tranquility of England, though under what specious pretences whatsoever; relieve the oppressed, hear the groans of poor prisoners in England; be pleased to reform the abuses of all professions, and if there be anyone that makes many poor to make a few rich, that suits not a Commonwealth. If He that strengthens your servants to fight, pleases to give you hearts to set upon these things in order to His glory, and the glory of your Commonwealth, besides the benefit England shall feel thereby, you shall shine forth to other nations, who shall emulate the glory of such a pattern and through the power of God turn into the like."[4]

Cromwell here asks Parliament to look to the restoration of law and order, peace and good government in the Commonwealth of England. He owns the hand of God in the victory but at once his mind turns to the need for peace and as he mentions in his letter after Naseby, 'to trust to God for the liberty of one's conscience and Parliament for the liberty for which we fight.'

But some of Cromwell's more personal correspondence, which was never intended for publication, reveals the deepest thoughts of his heart.

To his daughter, Bridget Ireton, he wrote:-

"London   25th October, 1646

Dear Daughter,

... And thus to be a seeker is to be of the best sect next to a finder; and such a one shall every faithful humble seeker be at the end. Happy seeker, happy finder. Whoever tasted that the Lord is gracious, without a sense of self, vanity and badness? Whoever tasted that graciousness of His, and could go less in desire and less than pressing after full enjoyment? Dear heart, press on; let not husband, let not anything cool thy affections after Christ. I hope he will be an occasion to inflame them. That which is best worthy of love in thy husband is that image of Christ he bears. Look on that and love it best; and all the rest for that. I pray for thee and him; do so for me."[5]

From Ireland he wrote to Lord Wharton on New Year's Day 1650. Lord Wharton, one of the Parliamentary Army Officers, had many doubts about the rightness of the execution of the King in the previous January. Cromwell wrote:-

"Cork   1st January, 1650

My Dear Friend, My Lord,

... It were a vain thing, by letter to dispute over your doubts, or to undertake to answer your objections. I have heard them all; and I have rest from trouble of them, and (of) what has risen in my own heart; for which I desire to be humbly thankful. I do not condemn your reasonings, I doubt them. It's easy to object to the glorious actings of God, if we look too much upon instruments ... Be not offended at the manner of God's working, perhaps no other way was left ... What if the Lord have witnessed His approbation and acceptance to this also, not only by signal outward acts, but to the heart also? ... Oh our deceitful hearts! Oh this pleasing world! How great it is to be the Lord's servant in any drudgery ... In all hazards His worst is far above the world's best. He makes us able in truth to say so; we cannot of ourselves. How hard a thing it is to reason ourselves up to the Lord's service, though it be so honourable; how easy to put ourselves out of it, where the flesh has so many advantages! ... The Lord direct your thoughts into the obedience of His will and give you rest and peace in the truth. Pray for your most true and affectionate servant in the Lord – Oliver Cromwell."[6]

This is a letter of good counsel – it shows us from Cromwell's own lips that the Lord had given him a sense of His approbation in the awful decision to try and execute Charles I. Cromwell was greatly tempted on his deathbed to wonder whether after all he was a castaway. His spiritual evidences were clouded and he called the Putitan minister, Thomas Goodwin, to his bedside to ask whether it was true – 'once in Him in Him for ever'. Goodwin assured him of the great truth – the final perseverance of the saints. His detractors have taken his darkness as evidence of a guilty conscience for his part in the execution of Charles I. But we have him writing here, a short time after the event, regarding his doubts and exercises of mind in this great matter, and he says, 'I have rest from the trouble of them ... for which I desire to be humbly thankful'. He had as he said, 'the Lord's approbation in his heart,' and this was all he wanted.

To his wife after Dunbar, he imparted his feelings in a more personal way than he had done to Speaker Lenthall, revealing his soul experiences before the battle:-

"Dunbar   4th September, 1650

My Dearest,

I have not leisure to write much ... The Lord hath showed us an exceeding mercy: who can tell how great it is. My weak faith hath been upheld. I have been in my inward man marvellously supported; though I assure thee, I grow an old man and feel the infirmities of age marvellously stealing upon me. Would my corruptions did as fast decrease. Pray on my behalf in the latter respect."[7]

Writing again to his wife from Edinburgh in April 1651 after a serious illness there, he said:-

"Edinburgh   12th April, 1651

My Dearest,

I praise the Lord I am increased in strength in the outward man; but that will not satisfy me except I get a heart to love and serve my heavenly Father better; and get more of the light of His countenance which is better than life, and more power over my corruptions: in these hopes I wait and am not without expectations of a gracious return. Pray for me; truly I do for thee daily and the dear family; and God Almighty bless you all with His spiritual blessings.

Mind poor Bettie of the Lord's great mercy. Oh I desire her not only to seek the Lord in her necessity, but in deed and in truth to turn to the Lord; and keep close to Him; and to take heed of a departing heart and of being a companion of worldly vanities and worldly company, which I doubt she is too much subject to. I earnestly and frequently pray for her and her husband. Truly they are dear to me, very dear; and I am in fear lest Satan should deceive them, knowing how weak our hearts are and how subtle the adversary is and what way the deceitfulness of our hearts and the vain world make for his temptations. The Lord give them truth of heart to Him. Let them seek Him in truth and they shall find Him. My love to the dear little ones. I pray for grace in them. I thank them for their letters, let me have them often ... Truly I am not able to get to write much. I am wearied and rest. Thine,   Oliver Cromwell."[8]

At this time Cromwell was fifty-two and considering his exertions mentally and physically in the past ten years, and the immense strain of the responsibility for the conduct of military affairs which rested on his shoulders, it is not surprising that he was taken ill. This letter from his sick bed to his wife and family reveals to us the loving father, the careful and praying parent watching over the spiritual welfare of his children and grandchildren. There is a transparent sincerity of purpose and feeling about this letter, which was never intended for the sight of any but his own family.

It does much to disarm the accusations made against his character by some of his opponents.

Finally two letters to his sons, Richard and Henry, reveal a father's concern for their welfare. Writing in 1650 to Richard who was living at the home of his wife at Hursley on the road between Winchester and Romsey, he said:-

"Carrick   2nd April, 1650

Dick Cromwell,

I take your letter kindly: I like expressions when they come plainly from the heart and are not strained nor affected.

I am persuaded it's the Lord's mercy to place you where you are: I wish you may own it and be thankful, fulfilling all relations to the glory of God. Seek the Lord and His face continually: let this be the business of your life and strength, and let all things be subservient and in order to this. You cannot find nor behold the face of God but in Christ; therefore labour to know God in Christ which the Scriptures make to be the sum of all, even life eternal. Because the true knowledge is not literal and speculative, but inward, transforming the mind to it. It's uniting to and participating of the Divine Nature. "Whereby are given unto us exceeding great and precious promises, that by these ye might be partakers of the divine nature, having escaped the corruption that is in the world through lust." [2 Peter 1. 4.] It's such a knowledge as Paul speaks of, "Yea doubtless and I count all things but loss for the excellency of the knowledge of Christ Jesus my Lord; for whom I have suffered the loss of all things and do count them but dung that I may win Christ and be found in Him, not having mine own righteous which is of the law, but that which is through the faith of Christ, the righteousness which is of God by faith: that I may know Him and the power of His resurrection and the fellow-ship of His sufferings, being made conformable unto His death." [Philippians 3. 8-10.] How little of this knowledge of Christ is there among us. My weak prayers shall be for you. Take heed of an inactive vain spirit ... Your loving father, Oliver Cromwell."[9]

The last sentence of this letter was a caution against idleness. Richard was living the life of a country squire on the lands of his father-in-law, Richard Mayor, the Squire of Hursley. His father saw great dangers spiritually in this life of ease and plenty.

The second letter, was written in 1656 to his son Henry, who was at that time Deputy Governor in Ireland. It reads:-

"Whitehall   21st April, 1656

Harry,

I have received your letters, and have also seen some from you to others, and am sufficiently satisfied of your burden and that if the Lord be not with you to enable you to bear it, you are in a very sad condition.

I am glad to hear what I have of your conduct, study still to be innocent and to answer every occasion, roll yourself upon God, which to do needs much grace. Cry to the Lord to give you a plain single heart . . . Know that uprightness will preserve you; in this be confident against men. Take heed of professing religion without the power; that will teach you to love all who are after the similitude of Christ. Take care of making it a business to be too hard with men who contest with you. Being over-concerned may bring you into a snare. I have to do with those poor men and am not without my exercise. I know they are weak, because they are so peremptory in judging others. I quarrel not with them but in their seeking to supplant others, which is done by some, first by branding them with anti-christianism and then by taking away their maintenance.

If the Lord do not sustain me I were undone: but I live, and shall live, to the good pleasure of His grace; I find mercy at need. The God of all grace keep you. I rest, your loving father, Oliver."[10]

Here we see Cromwell urging his son to a kindly, cautious handling of those who opposed him in his management of Irish affairs and to avoid hasty judgements of others. It shows us what a liberal, magnanimous spirit Cromwell had towards those who opposed him. He offered good advice in his words, "take heed of professing religion without the power." There was much profession of religion in his day, but Cromwell's mind centred on the real as opposed to the false, and nothing but divine realities satisfied his soul.

Secondly it is possible to learn much about Cromwell from a consideration of his speeches. Delivered with his usual spontaneity, they reveal much of the mind and heart of the man. The first extract concerns liberty of conscience, a subject always dear to Cromwell. It is part of a speech made to the First Protectorate Parliament on 12th September, 1654. Remembering the times in which he lived, that the Civil Wars had developed through religious intolerance of Charles I and were followed by a similar intolerance of his son Charles II in England and Scotland, this speech shows how far ahead of his times Cromwell was in thought and action, for during his period of rule Catholics, Jews and Protestants of all kinds enjoyed a far greater measure of religious liberty than ever before, so long as they did not interfere with the government of the country. I quote:-

"Is not liberty of conscience a fundamental? So long as there is liberty of conscience for the Supreme Magistrate (i.e. Cromwell) to exercise his conscience in erecting what form of Church Government he is satisfied he should set up, why should he not give it to others? Liberty of conscience is a natural right; and he that would have it ought to give it; having liberty to settle what he likes for the public. Indeed that hath been one of the vanities of our contests. Every sect saith: 'Oh give me liberty!' But give him it, and to his power he will not yield it to anybody else. Where is our ingenuousness? Truly that's a thing that ought to be very reciprocal. The magistrate hath his supremacy and may settle religion according to his conscience. And 'as for the people,' I may say it to you, I can say it: All the money in the nation would not have tempted men to fight upon such an account as they have engaged in, if they had not had hopes of liberty better than they had from Episcopacy, or than would have been afforded them from Scottish Presbytery, or an English either, if it had made such steps, or been as sharp or rigid as it threatened when it was first set up. It ought to be so. It is for us and the generations to come. And if there be an absoluteness in the imposer, without fitting allowances and exceptions from the rule, we shall have our people driven into the wilderness, as they were, when those poor and afflicted people, that forsook their estates and inheritances here, where they lived plentifully and comfortably, for the enjoyment of their liberty, were necessitated to go into a vast howling wilderness in New England – where they have for liberty's sake, stript themselves of all their comfort and the full enjoyment they had, embracing rather the loss of friends and want, than to be ensnared and in bondage."[11]

Cromwell felt great affection for the Pilgrim Fathers. It seems probable that he himself had considered leaving the shores of this island at one period to seek freedom of conscience abroad, but had stayed here to fight for the maintenance of freedom in this land, and as he says in this speech, 'It is for us and the generations to come!'

In another speech Cromwell made to the Second Protectorate Parliament on 20th January, 1658, the year of his death, he scans the work of his life, and reveals what he thought were the causes of the Civil Wars and the benefits obtained from them.

"My Lords and Gentlemen of the House of Commons,

I meet you here in this capacity by the advice and petition of this present parliament; after so much expense of blood and treasure, to search and try what blessings God hath in store for these nations. I cannot but with gladness of heart remember and acknowledge the labour and industry that is past, which hath been spent upon a business worthy of the best men and the best Christians.

It is very well known unto you all what difficulties we have passed through and what we are now arrived to. We hope we may say, we have arrived at where we aimed at, if not at that which is much beyond our expectations. The state of this cause, and the quarrel, what that was at the first, you all very well know; I am persuaded most of you have been actors in it: it was the maintaining of the liberty of these nations; our civil liberties as men, our spiritual liberties as Christians. I shall not much look back; but rather say one word concerning the state and condition we are all now in.

You very well know ... after the beginning of the War ... that for some succession of time, designs were laid to innovate upon the civil rights of the nation and to innovate in matters of religion. And those very persons that a man would have thought should have had the least hand in meddling with civil things (bishops) did justify them all ... in pulpits, in presses, and otherwise. Which was verily thought would have been a very good shelter to them, to innovate upon us in matters of religion also. And so to innovate as to cut out the core and power and heart of life of all religion by bringing on us a company of poisonous Popish ceremonies and imposing them upon those that were accounted the Puritans of the Nation and professors of religion among us – driving them to seek their bread in a howling wilderness, as was instanced to our friends who were forced to fly for Holland, New England, almost anywhither to find liberty for their conscience.

You see that the Petition and Advice that brought me hither hath not through a little difficulty, restored us both in point of civil liberty as we are men, and liberty for all those that are of the Protestant profession amongst us, who enjoy a freedom to worship God according to their consciences.

Now if this thing hath been the state and the sum of our quarrel and of these Ten Years Wars, wherein we have been exercised; and that the good hand of God, for we are to attribute it to no other, hath brought this business thus home to us as it is stated in the petition and advice – I think we have all cause to bless God and the nations have cause to bless Him.

I well remember I did a little touch upon the Eighty-fifth Psalm when I spoke to you in the beginning of this Parliament, which expresseth well that that we may say, as truly and as well as it was said of old by the penman of that Psalm. The first verse is an acknowledgement to God that He hath been favourable unto His land, and had brought back the captivity of His people; and that He had pardoned all their iniquities and covered all their sins and taken away all His wrath; and indeed of the sense of these unspeakable mercies, blessings and deliverances out of captivity, pardoning national sins and national iniquities. Pardoning as God pardoneth the man who He justifieth. He breaks through and overlooks iniquity; and pardoneth because He will pardon. And sometimes God pardoneth nations so – and if the enjoyment of our present peace and other mercies may be witnesses for to us – we feel and we see them every day.

The greatest demonstration of His favour and love appears to us in this: that He hath given us peace; and the blessings of peace, to wit, the enjoyment of our liberties, civil and spiritual. And I remember well the Church falls into prayer, and praises, great expectations of future mercies and much thankfulness for the enjoyment of present mercies; and breaks into this expression: "Surely salvation is nigh unto them that fear Him; that glory may dwell in our land." In the beginning He calls it His land; "Thou hast been favourable to Thy land." Truly I hope this (England) is His land, and in some sense it may be given out that it is God's land. And he that hath the weakest knowledge and the worst memory can easily tell that we are the redeemed people. We were a redeemed people when first God was pleased to look favourably upon us, out of the hands of Popery, in that never to be forgotten Reformation, that most significant and greatest the nation hath felt and tasted. I would but touch upon that, and but a touch: how hath God redeemed us as we stand this day. Not from trouble and sorrow and anger only, but into a blessed and happy estate and condition, comprehensive of all the interest of every member, every individual; of those mercies, as you very well see.

And then in what sense is it our land; through this grace and favour of God, that He hath vouchsafed unto us and bestowed upon us, with the Gospel, peace and rest out of ten years war; and given us what we would desire! Nay, who could have forethought, when we were plunged in the midst of our troubles, that ever the people of God should have liberty to worship God without fear of enemies? Which is the very acknowledgement of the promise of Christ that He would deliver His from fear of enemies, that they might worship Him in holiness and in righteousness all the days of their life.

This is the portion that God hath given us; and I trust we shall forever heartily acknowledge it. The Church goes on there and makes her boast yet farther; "His salvation is nigh them that fear Him, that glory may dwell in our land". His glory; not carnal, nor anything related thereto: this glory of a free possession of the Gospel; this is that we may glory in. And it is said farther, "Mercy and truth are met together; righteousness and peace have kissed each other." And it shall be such righteousness as comes down from heaven: "Truth shall grow out of the earth and righteousness shall come down from heaven." Here is the truth of all; here is the righteousness of God under the notion of righteousness confirming our abilities, answerable to the truth that He hath in the Gospel revealed towards us. And the Psalm closeth with this: "Righteousness shall go before Him and shall set us in the way of His steps"; that righteousness, that mercy, that love and that kindness which we have seen, and been made partakers of from the Lord, it shall be our guide to teach us to know the right and the good way; which is to tread in the steps of mercy, righteousness and goodness that our God hath walked before us in.

We have a peace this day! I believe in my very heart, you all think the things that I speak to you this day. I am sure you have cause."[12]

Men like Cromwell, of his generation, had witnessed the sufferings in times of religious persecution, especially from the High Church Party under Archbishop Laud, and this speech and the previous one, show how much they valued political and religious liberty, and treasured the peace they possessed.

The last extract comes from a speech made to the First Protectorate Parliament on 22nd January, 1655. He said:-

"Supposing this cause or this business must be carried on, either it is of God or of man. If it be of man, I would I had never touched it with a finger. If I had not had a hope fixed in me that this cause and this business is of God, I would many years ago have run from it. If it be of God, He will bear it up. If it be of man, it will tumble; as everything that hath been of man since the world began hath done. And what are all our histories, and other traditions of actions in former times, but God manifesting Himself, that He hath shaken and tumbled down and trampled upon everything that He had not planted? And as this is, so the all-wise God deal with it. If this be of human structure and invention, and it be an old plotting and contrivance to bring things to this issue, and that they are not the births of providence, then they will tumble. But if the Lord take pleasure in England, and if He will do us good, He is able to bear us up! Let the difficulties be whatsoever they will, we shall in His strength be able to encounter with them. And I bless God I have been inured to difficulties; and I never found God failing when I trusted Him."[13]

What wonderful words are those to echo out in the Houses of Parliament, "I never found God failing when I trusted Him".

In the last century God has honoured Cromwell and raised his name from much of the obloquy in which it has lain since his death. In the eighteenth century, men like Augustus Toplady, the hymn writer, had little or no time for Cromwell – but in 1845, Thomas Carlyle published the letters and speeches of Cromwell, which, though spiritually showing no real understanding of Cromwell's religion, gave to the world for the first time a collected edition of his writings and utterances. This, as nothing else could have done, vindicated Cromwell from the false charges, which had been current for so long. These letters and speeches reveal Cromwell's own words, the outpourings of his heart. The whole of his life was guided by a constant contact with His Heavenly Father through prayer and reading the Word. Like so many of his great contemporaries, his whole writings are permeated with gospel language; the words of the great book, either the Geneva Version of 1560 or the 1611 Authorized Version, which were his constant companion. This Book, through the power of the Holy Spirit, was the food of his soul.

What then about the charges made against him of desecrating Churches and massacring the Irish population of Drogheda. The other charges can be left, because his writings amply repel the charge of hypocrisy. If that charge is true, Cromwell is an absolute impostor; but an examination of his writings and speeches show what a sincere man he was. The charges of usurper and dictator are equally dispelled when one examines his efforts to establish a freely elected Parliament – all of which failed, not through any lack of effort on his part. He truly said on one occasion, "And know, I sought not this place. I speak it before God, angels, and men: I did not. You sought me for it and you brought me to it." (Speech to the Second Protectorate Parliament, 25th January, 1658.)[14]

What of Drogheda then? Tom Reilly in his book *Cromwell – An Honourable Enemy* [1999 p. 85] has given an entirely new assessment of civilian losses in Cromwell's Irish Campaign of 1649, showing that there were no mass burials of civilians at that time and that most of those who were killed were armed combatants. He says, 'So far we have no solid proof that any unarmed civilians had died at the hands of Cromwell [in the siege of Drogheda]. Indeed, to date [Sept. 1649], no one man had died in the cause of Irish nationalism. There was of course no shortage of those who had died giving their lives for the defence of the English monarchy.' We are faced with the difficulties of a Christian soldier. The British Army has had many Christian soldiers – General Gordon in the nineteenth century; Sir William Dobbie in the twentieth century. A Christian companion of Cromwell was Henry Ireton, for not all the Parliamentary Generals of the Civil War gave evidence of being truly converted men. Cromwell received his appointment to Ireland in March 1649 and eventually sailed for that country in July, landing in Dublin on 15th July. He was to restore order in Ireland, which had been in a state of rebellion since 1641. It is estimated that in the Irish uprising in that year 10-15,000 Protestants had been killed in places such as Portadown. His opponents were not entirely Irish Catholics, but also consisted of Protestant and Catholic Royalists, united under the command of the Marquis of Ormonde. They had been defeated at Rathmines by a Parliamentary army under Colonel Michael Jones just two weeks before Cromwell's arrival. Now unwilling and unable to face Cromwell in the field, the Royalists and Irish resorted to siege warfare.

The Governor and garrison of Drogheda were mainly Royalists, under the command of Sir Arthur Aston, a Catholic, a former governor of Oxford in 1644. On 3rd September, 1649 Cromwell's Army of 10,000 camped before Drogheda, which had a garrison of about 3,000 troops. On the 9th Cromwell sent a summons to Aston to surrender the town, and he refused. By the laws of war as then understood, when a fortified town refused the summons of surrender, the lives of all found in arms after the assault were held to be forfeit. On the 11th a breach was made in the walls and after an unsuccessful attempt to break in, Cromwell himself leapt forward and led his troops into the town. He says in a despatch after the battle, "In the heat of action, I forbade them (his men) to spare any that were in arms in the town; and I think that night they put to the sword about 2,000 men." Others who retreated into a church steeple and refused to surrender were burnt out. Every friar in the town was killed and civilians fell in the confusion of battle.

Professor Gardiner remarks that Cromwell was probably the only man in the victorious army who imagined that this signal punishment required any excuse at all. In later years this military strategy of an overwhelming assault with severity, aimed at frightening other garrisons to surrender has been equally employed just as in the seventeenth century. The Duke of Wellington refers to it as accepted practice in his day. Cromwell in his despatch to Parliament says, "I am persuaded that this is a righteous judgement of God upon these barbarous wretches, who have imbued their hands with so much innocent blood, and that it will tend to prevent the effusion of blood for the future; which are the satisfactory grounds to such actions, which otherwise cannot but work remorse and regret." Such an action undertaken by a nominally Christian general in a conflict which had no religious overtones would have provoked little attention; but considering Cromwell's Puritan background [John Owen, the Puritan divine was with him in Ireland as his chaplain] Royalists and Catholics have made much of the apparent disparity between his Christian profession and his conduct at the siege of Drogheda.

From a military point of view the Parliamentary Army had been sent to Ireland to recover it as a rebellious colony and prevent Charles II from using it as a jumping-off ground for his army to recover his throne in England. Later Charles II had used Scotland for this purpose and Cromwell's Army had moved there to defeat him first at the battle of Dunbar and then in England at the battle of Worcester. The original colonisation of Ireland had not been the work of Oliver Cromwell or Charles I, though Charles I's minister in Ireland, Thomas Wentworth, had ruled the country prior to the Civil Wars with a reign of terror. Colonisation had begun in the reign of Henry II and been carried on in the reign of Henry VIII, with the colonisation of Ulster completed in the reign of Elizabeth I. History shows consistently that colonisation has been the cause of conflict and loss of life and Ireland is no exception to this. In the massacres of Drogheda and Wexford, Cromwell's name has become synony-mous with the evils of colonisation. In leading the Parliamentary Army he became caught up in a situation not of his own making. In attempting to eliminate Ireland as a Royalist jumping-off ground for the re-conquest of England by the Royalists, he recovered Ireland for the Parliamentary Government. Cromwell himself wholly acquiesced in this policy. His own son, Henry Cromwell became a leading administrator in Ireland.

Finally there is the general charge made against Cromwell and the Parliamentary side of damaging cathedrals and churches. There is no doubt that damage was done to church buildings of a considerable nature during the Civil War. But it is equally clear that Cromwell did not travel in person to every part of the country during the War. It is a fact that troops under his command were highly disciplined and on occasions he executed his own soldiers for looting. Modern historical research is revealing more and more that he was a moderate man, who tried in a day of bigotry to exercise toleration in his dealing with others and wished for a degree of religious toleration between those who differed. He found it impossible to extend this view of toleration to Catholics, principally because the Catholic church had throughout the Reformation times and onwards been so deeply involved in politics, in such events as the execution of the Marian martyrs, the Armada, the Gunpowder Plot etc. Thus though his views on freedom of speech and freedom of religion were not as complete as ours, yet he led this country towards that goal. Regarding Cromwell's personal responsibility for damaging church buildings, Peter Gaunt in his biography of Cromwell says, 'Such cleansing of churches by stripping out images and ornate decoration as did occur in the mid-seventeenth century was the policy of Parliament and Parliament's local agents; very little iconoclasm was undertaken in person or by troops under Cromwell's direct and immediate command.'

This assertion can be judged in connection with the City of Winchester. A Royalist writer, refers to the entry of the Parliamentary Army into Winchester in 1642, soon after the battle of Edgehill. This does not refer specifically to Cromwell, who was not in command of these forces, but it shows the sort of ill-founded charges made against the Parliamentary side. The Royalist writer says, "They forced their way into the Cathedral, invading God

Himself as well as His profession . . . with colours flying, their drums beating, their matches fixed, and . . . some of their troops of horse also accompanied them on their march and rode up through the body of the Church and the Chancel until they came to the altar". Here they are said to have swept away all the ornaments, ruined the Chantries, "and break in pieces Queen Mary's chair in which she sat at her marriage with Philip of Spain". The answer to these charges is simply this. The altar and reredos had already been dealt with by the Anglicans themselves nearly a century before. The Chantries had been reduced to the same state as they now are at the same period; that is during the Reformation, principally in the reign of Edward VI 1547-1553. And Mary's chair is still intact in the Cathedral today. It has also been alleged by a Canon of the Cathedral, writing in 1911 and generally repeated since then, that between 1642 and 1646 priceless manuscripts were taken from the Cathedral Library by the Parliamentarians. But ten or fifteen years ago, the Library of the Cathedral acquired a list of its manuscripts, made in 1620, and that list shows its possessions then were substantially the same as its possessions now. This raises a misunderstanding which frequently occurs; namely the confusing of Oliver Cromwell with Thomas Cromwell. Thomas Cromwell was the Vicar General of Henry VIII and organiser in 1536 of the Dissolution of the Monasteries. He had a hand in the dispersion of many of the medieval libraries and valuable works of art of the churches of his day; so that it is often possible for the blame attaching to him, to be mistakenly attributed to Oliver. A recent book entitled *Destruction in the English Civil Wars* by Stephen Porter [1997 Sutton paperback] gives an account of the extent and type of destruction in the Civil Wars and helps to disprove the idea that Cromwell was responsible for all the damage.

Oliver's connection with Winchester came in September 1645, shortly after the great Parliamentary victory at Naseby. Winchester was then in the hands of the Royalists and he came to subdue the city and its castle. He arrived before the city in the afternoon of Sunday, 28th September and sent the Mayor a demand for entrance, promising to save the city and its inhabitants. The Mayor declined to surrender, saying that the city was under the command of the Royalist governor of the castle, Lord Ogle. Cromwell, who was camping on the open downs to the West of the City, near the ancient earthwork known as 'Oliver's Battery,' fired one of the city gates and without much difficulty entered the city with three regiments of foot and 2,000 horse. The castle was then summoned to surrender and refused. Cannon now played on the walls of the castle and by the following Saturday had made a wide breach. At this point, after a successful outward attack by the Royalists, Lord Ogle decided to ask for terms before he was wiped out with his forces. These terms were agreed, the castle surrendered and the garrison was allowed to march away to Woodstock near Oxford. Cromwell declared at the time that "all officers, gentlemen, clergy and inhabitants of the city of Winchester ... may be free from all violence and injury of the Parliamentary forces," and he kept his word, for of six Parliamentary soldiers who disobeyed this decree, one was hung and the other five sent to Oxford to the Parliamentary Governor to be dealt with. Winchester certainly has good cause to remember the justice and mercy of Oliver Cromwell. He was a much maligned man, but for many he is still regarded as a great soldier and a statesman. Let John Milton, the poet of the Civil War, have the final word on Oliver Cromwell in his famous sonnet.

Cromwell our chief of men, who through a cloud
Not of war only, but detraction rude,
Guided by faith and matchless fortitude,
To peace and truth thy glorious way hast plough'd,
And on the neck of crown'd fortune proud
Hast reared God's trophies, and his work pursued,
While Darwen stream, with blood of Scots imbued,
And Dunbar field resounds thy praises loud,
And Worcester's laureat wreath. Yet much remains
To conquer still; peace hath her victories
No less renown'd than war; new foes arise
Threat'ning to bind our souls with secular chains:
Help us to save free conscience from the paw
Of hireling wolves, whose gospel is their maw.

Notes

1. W.C. Abbott (ed.) *The Writings & Speeches of Oliver Cromwell* (4 vols, Harvard, 1937-47; Oxford University Press reprint edition, 1989). Vol I p. 96-7.

2. Abbott, vol. I, pp. 287-8.

3. Abbott, vol. I, p. 360.

4. Abbott, vol. II, pp. 324-5

5. Abbott, vol. I, p. 416.

6. Abbott, vol. II, pp. 189-90.

7. Abbott, vol. II, p. 329.

8. Abbott, vol. II, p. 412.

9. Abbott, vol. II, p. 237

10. Abbott, vol. IV, p.146.

11. Abbott, vol. III, pp. 435-39.

12. Abbott, vol. IV, p. 705.

13. Abbott, vol. III, pp. 580-93.

14. I. Roots, *Speeches of Oliver Cromwell* (Dent, 1989), pp 168-73.

Bibliography

The above lecture was originally given at Winchester at "The Wessex Conference" in 1964. It was published first in 1969 and reprinted in 1972. Reprinted now, it has been considerably revised and extended.

When Cromwell's name was rehabilitated in the 19th century, the principal sources were the works of S.R. Gardiner and C.H. Firth and the *Letters and Speeches of Oliver Cromwell* [1845] by Thomas Carlyle. A fine edition of Carlyle's work was published in 1904 in three volumes with notes by S.C. Lomas and an excellent introduction by C.H. Firth. The leading writers on Oliver Cromwell in the period 1950-60 were Dr Maurice Ashley and C.V. Wedgewood. Other writers on the military aspects of Cromwell's life were Colonel A. Burne and Brigadier Peter Young. Two biographies which took particular note of the spiritual side of Cromwell's life were *The Protector* by Dr H.H. Merle D'Aubigne, (Edinburgh, 1874) and *Oliver Cromwell – A Study in Personal Religion* by Dr R.F. Horton (London 1897.) In more recent times Dr Robert S. Paul has written on the spiritual side of Cromwell's character in his book *The Lord Protector* (Lutterworth Press, 1958)

Between 1937-1947 W.C. Abbott published an edition of *The Writings and Speeches of Oliver Cromwell* (4 vols, Cambridge, Mass.) This was reprinted by Oxford University Press 1989 but is now out of print as a set. A [rare] collection of *The Speeches of Oliver Cromwell* edited by C.L. Stainer was published by Oxford University Press in 1901. The 26 most important speeches, largely from the Stainer edition, were edited by Professor Ivan Roots and published (London, 1989).

During the 1980's A. Blair Worden published an important group of articles on the theme of Cromwell and religion: *Toleration and the Cromwellian Protectorate*, in W.J. Sheils, (ed.), *Persecution and Toleration: Studies in Church History* XXI (Oxford, 1984); *Providence and Politics in Cromwellian England* in *Past and Present* 109 (1985); *Oliver Cromwell and the Sin of Achan*, in D. Beales and G. Best (eds), *History, Society and the Churches* (Cambridge 1985). John Morrill, Professor of History at Cambridge and President of the Cromwellian Association, says in 'Suggestions for further reading,' in his book, *Oliver Cromwell and the English Revolution* (Longman 1990), (4th Impression 1995), 'The most important recent work on Cromwell has undoubtedly been that of Blair Worden, who is writing what is certain to be the outstanding biography of him written this century.'

John Morrill's book mentioned above was a landmark itself in Cromwellian studies. Published in 1990 and edited by him it consists of a series of essays of an exceptionally high standard on various themes. In the first two chapters Morrill gives first a concise introduction to the character of Cromwell and then pioneers new ground on his early life, examining Cromwell's role in the Long Parliament. Other essays include *Cromwell and the Long Parliament* by J.S.A Adamson, *Cromwell as a Soldier* by Austin Woolrych, *The Lord Protector, 1653-1658* by Derek Hirst, *Cromwell, Scotland and Ireland* by David Stevenson, *Cromwell's Religion* by J.C. Davis, *Oliver Cromwell and the Godly Nation* by Anthony Fletcher, and *Oliver Cromwell and English Political Thought* by Johann Sommerville. Morrill concludes the series with an essay examining the views that Cromwell's contemporaries had of him, which were printed in his lifetime.

In 1991, Barry Coward, Reader in History at Birbeck College, London University published a study of Cromwell in the Longmans series *Profiles in Power*. This book now in its fifth impression, is an excellent biography. Coward says in his introduction, 'I had always thought that the main characteristic of Oliver Cromwell's career was its inconsistency... Yet from a point in the early 1640s onwards, it will be argued, there is a *consistent* thread running through his career.' Other useful articles on Cromwell can be found in *Cromwelliana* , The Annual Journal of the Cromwell Association, past and present copies of which can be obtained from the Honorary Secretary, Dr Judith D.Hutchinson, 52 East View, Barnet, Herts. EN5 5TN. In 1996, Peter Gaunt published a new biography of Oliver Cromwell and in 1999 Tom Reilly published his research on Cromwell's Irish Campaign in a book entitled *Cromwell – An Honourable Enemy* which dealt with primary material concerning that period. In 2001 J.C. Davis, Professor of English History at East Anglia University published a study of Cromwell examining his reputation down the ages, his stature as a soldier, politician, state-builder, and man of God.